CONTENTS

Introduction	4
The land	6
Weather, plants and animals	8
Towns and cities	10
Living in Moscow	12
Farming in Russia	14
Living in the country	16
Russian shops	18
Russian food	20
Made in Russia	22
Getting around	24
Sports and holidays	26
Festivals and arts	28
Factfile	30
Glossary	31
Index	32

INTRODUCTION

St Basil's Cathedral, in Moscow. It was finished in 1560 and is a big **tourist** attraction.

WHERE IS RUSSIA?

Russia stretches east from Europe until it almost touches Alaska. It is a huge country. If you cross Russia you cross 11 time zones. The UK has only one.

Russia has borders with lots of other countries from Finland to China. It has many different seas around its coastlines.

City Population
- ○ over 1,000,000
- ● over 500,000
- ● capital

0   500   1000 km

Communist Russia was made up of over 100 countries, each with their own language.

RUSSIA'S HISTORY

At first, Russia was ruled by tsars, who were like kings. In 1917, a **revolution** replaced the tsars with a **communist government** and Russia was called the USSR. In 1991 the USSR split up. The biggest new country is the Russian Federation.

The Russian flag changed as rulers changed. This is the new flag.

THE LAND

Height in metres
- over 1000
- 500–1000
- 200–500
- 0–200

0   500   1000 km

ARCTIC OCEAN

PACIFIC OCEAN

RUSSIA

Kamchatka Peninsula

R. Yenisey

R. Lena

R. Volga

Black Sea

Mt Elbrus ▲5633

Caucasus Mountains

Caspian Sea

Lake Baikal

MOUNTAINS

Russia has lots of mountains. The highest mountains are in the Caucasus Mountains, in the south-west. There are lots of **volcanoes** in the east of the country. Many of them still **erupt**.

One of the 22 active volcanoes in eastern Russia. One of them has erupted over 70 times since 1967.

A bridge across the widest part of the River Volga. The Volga is the longest river in Russia.

THE STEPPES

In southern Russia there is a large, flat **plain** called the steppes. The soil here is good for growing crops, and it is easy to use farm machinery on the flat land.

RIVERS AND LAKES

Russia has some of the longest, widest rivers in the world. Most of these rivers flow north, to the Arctic Ocean.

There are many lakes in Russia. Some of them, like Lake Balaton in the warm south, have become holiday resorts. Lake Baikal, in Siberia, is too cold for that. But it is the deepest lake in the world.

The River Volga flows into the Caspian Sea. This is not a sea at all, but the largest lake in the world.

7

WEATHER, PLANTS AND ANIMALS

Murmansk is in the far north of Russia. In December and January the sun never rises. The temperature is below freezing for half of the year.

THE WEATHER

Russia is so big that there are places where the temperature hardly ever gets above freezing and places where it is so hot it is almost a **desert**.

The size of Russia is one reason for the difference. The other reason is that northern Russia is so far north that the sun, even in summer, is so low in the sky it doesn't really warm the ground up.

PLANTS AND ANIMALS

The far north of Russia has tundra where only moss and small plants can grow in the cold. Polar bears and reindeer live there.

South of the tundra is the taiga – a huge forest of **coniferous** trees. Bears, wolves and elk live here. South of this, trees like oak and birch grow, where there are wild boar and mink. Then there is a high, flat area once covered in grasses – the steppes, where there are polecats. The areas furthest south are hot and dry.

There are a few tigers in Siberia. But they are hunted for their skins and are dying out.

The taiga is a huge forest that stretches across Russia. The trees are cut down and taken to factories.

TOWNS AND CITIES

Lots of **tourists** come to visit St Petersburg each year. They come to look at the beautiful old buildings and **canals**.

In 1900, one out of every four people in Russia lived in towns and cities. Now it is three out of every four.

ST PETERSBURG

St Petersburg is the second largest city in Russia. It used to be the capital city, until 1918. It was built in 1703, by Tsar Peter the Great. It is an important port.

The names of some Russian towns and cities, even streets and squares, have been changed by the new rulers.

MOSCOW

Moscow became the capital city of Russia in 1918. Moscow has an old centre, but has lots of new offices, factories and flats, too. Red Square is in the centre of the city. It is called this because the Russian for 'red' and 'beautiful' are the same.

FACTORY TOWNS

A lot of new towns in Russia were built to mine coal and oil, or to make iron and steel. There are also **nuclear power** plants. Many of these cities make a lot of air and water **pollution**.

Most people in Moscow live in small flats in new tower blocks like these. They all look the same.

LIVING IN MOSCOW

THE OSHUROV FAMILY

Anatoly and Marina Oshurov live in a flat in Moscow. They have one girl, Anita, who is twelve.

Anatoly works for a company that sells fruit juice and milk. He works on a computer.

THE FAMILY'S DAY

Anatoly and Marina work full-time. Anita goes to school. Marina works for a company that helps people to leave Russia and move to other countries. Before 1991, it was hard for people to leave Russia. Now it is easier.

The family live on the top floor of this building. There is no lift. They have to use the stairs.

MEALTIMES

The family eat together most evenings. They like beetroot soup, pancakes and salad. They try to eat balanced meals with meat and vegetables but food costs a lot and there is not much choice. The family spend a lot of time shopping – there are often queues. They go to local shops and markets.

Anita's classroom at school. There is homework every night.

The flat is very small. The family eat in the kitchen.

FARMING IN RUSSIA

These machines are harvesting wheat. Only big, government-run farms can buy machines like this.

GROWING WHEAT

Wheat grows well in the flat steppes. The soil and the weather are good. The land is flat, so farmers can use big machines to plough the soil and cut the wheat. But sometimes the farmers cannot grow enough to feed all the people, so there are food shortages.

GOVERNMENT FARMS

Before 1991, the **government** ran all the farms. They chose what to grow and what prices to charge. The government still owns most big farms, which grow wheat, barley, oats and potatoes.

OTHER FARMS

Now farmers can run their own farms. They are mostly small and near a town. Usually, they grow vegetables and fruit to sell in the local market.

Only 14% of the land in Russia is good for farming. The rest is too cold or steep, or is already built on.

Soldiers help collect potatoes on a government-run farm.

LIVING IN THE COUNTRY

The family's house is bigger than a flat in the city. It has five rooms. They have a TV, a stereo and a washing machine.

THE DMITREIEV FAMILY

Sergey and Olga Dmitreiev live in a village in the south-west of Russia. They have one boy, Andrey (who is nine) and one girl, Misha (who is two). In the village, everyone works on the same farm.

The villagers do most of their own repairs on the farm machines.

THE FAMILY'S DAY

Sergey ploughs the soil, or drives the harvester. Olga looks after the cows. Andrey goes to school in the village.

Olga helps Andrey with his homework in the evenings.

EARNING A BIT MORE

The family have a garden where they grow cabbages, tomatoes, cucumbers, beetroot and apples. If they grow more than they can eat, they sell it to other villagers.

MEALTIMES

The family eat breakfast together in the morning. They eat their main meal in the evening. Sergey and Olga grow a lot of the vegetables they need. They can buy bread and meat at shops in the village.

RUSSIAN SHOPS

CHANGING TIMES

Before 1991, the **communist government** ran the shops. There was basic food (like bread and potatoes) at a set price. There were often long queues. It was hard to get things like clothes and shoes.

Now anyone can open a shop with their own prices. There are more things to buy but very few people can afford them.

A new shopping arcade. Only rich people, like the woman here, can afford to buy things in these grand shops.

In Russian shops you pay first. You get a ticket for the things you want. Then you swap the ticket for the things you have paid for.

MARKETS

There are street markets all over Russia. They are often the only place where you can buy fruit and vegetables.

Farmers, who grow more than they need, sell the food to passers-by. Because there are often food shortages, people who have food to sell can charge a lot.

*Some shops, especially those selling things to **tourists**, do not take Russian money. They ask to be paid in foreign money.*

19

RUSSIAN FOOD

These people have wrapped up warm for a barbecue. This is as hot as the weather gets!

TRADITIONAL FOOD

Russia has lots of traditional foods, because it was once lots of different countries. Borsch (beetroot soup), blinis (pancakes), tabaka (chicken with cabbage and prunes) and strogonov (beef with onion, mushrooms and sour cream) are all traditional foods.

Many adults in Russia drink vodka. It is made from potatoes and is very cheap.

ORDINARY FOOD AND DRINK

Most people cook with what they can find in the shops and markets. They change recipes around to fit what they have got. They drink black tea and vodka.

SPECIAL FOOD AND DRINK

Not much Russian food is sold to other countries. But Russian vodka is drunk all over the world. Most of the caviar from Russia is sold to other countries. It is very expensive. It is fish eggs.

This family are eating soup, bread, vegetables from their garden and spicy sausage.

MADE IN RUSSIA

These tractors will go to people who cut down and saw up trees for export to other countries.

Russia is starting to sell more **exports** to other countries. Russia did not export much at all before 1991.

FACTORIES

Before 1991, factories had to make what the **government** told them to. They made tanks, tractors, railway trucks, ships and also things like shoes and furniture.

Russia mines more gold than any other country in the world.

Factories like this metal factory cause a lot of air and water pollution. Piles of waste build up, too.

CHANGES

Since 1991 the government has tried to change what factories make. They want them to make washing machines and microwaves, not tanks. They also want them to be more careful about **pollution**.

The government wants factories to make things for export. This will make money for Russia. They will be able to sell **goods** at cheaper prices, because workers in Russia earn a lot less than workers in other countries in Europe.

GETTING AROUND

Irkutsk station. Most people travel (or send goods) long distances by train, not road.

Travel in Russia can be a problem. Long distances and bad weather cause delays.

TRAINS

You can travel right across Russia on the Trans-Siberia railway. There are smaller railway lines all across the country.

ROADS

The best roads in Russia are in the west of the country, linking Moscow and other cities like St Petersburg. Many roads in the rest of Russia are gravel or dirt tracks and are often blocked with snow.

In the Siberian winter, the rivers freeze so hard that drivers use them as roads when roads are blocked!

CITY TRAVEL

It is easier to travel in the cities than outside them. Most cities have good **public transport**, because only a few people own cars. Buses and underground railways are cheap and quick. With less traffic there is less **pollution**.

Moscow underground stations have been decorated in different ways. This one looks very grand. Others look very modern.

25

SPORTS AND HOLIDAYS

SPORTS

Russian sports training is very good. They have good football and ice hockey teams. Russian athletes often do well at the Olympic Games.

Most Russian cities have sports grounds, swimming pools and ice rinks that are cheap to use.

Now that Russia is making more links with other countries, sports like tennis and golf are becoming popular. But they are expensive and there are not many places to play.

Reindeer racing is popular in Murmansk, in the north of Russia.

This dacha (weekend home) is very grand. Most dachas are not as decorated as this.

TIME OFF

City people often stay with relatives in the country at weekends. Some have their own dachas – small wooden houses with tiny gardens.

HOLIDAYS

Only a few Russians can afford to go to another country on holiday. Mostly, they go to a different part of Russia. They may go to the north for skiing or to a hot holiday resort in the south.

FESTIVALS AND ARTS

Priests from the Russian Orthodox Church celebrate Easter. This public celebration could not have happened under communist rule.

RELIGIOUS FESTIVALS

The **communist government** did not believe in religion. The Russian Orthodox Church had to hold its services in secret. People now celebrate these festivals again.

OTHER FESTIVALS

The biggest non-religious festival is held on 1 May. It is International Solidarity Day – to celebrate Russian workers.

The Russian State Library in Moscow has more than 30 million books.

ARTS

Russia has many museums, art galleries and theatres. Russian art will become more well-known as Russia has more and more contact with other countries.

Russian music and ballet are already famous. The Moscow State Circus performs all over the world. There are lots of circuses that travel all over Russia.

This parade is to celebrate the end of the Second World War. The parade is held on 9 May each year.

29

RUSSIA FACTFILE

People

People from Russia are called Russians.

Capital city

The capital city is Moscow.

Largest cities

Moscow is the largest city. Nearly 9 million people live in Moscow.
St Petersburg is the second largest city and Nizhniy Novgorod is the third largest.

Head of country

The head of Russia is called the president.

Population

There are about 150 million people living in Russia.

Money

People use roubles and kopecks. 1 rouble = 100 kopecks

Language

Most people speak Russian but some speak Tartar, Ukrainian, Chuvash or other Russian languages.

Religion

The most common religions in Russia are Christianity, Islam and Buddhism.

GLOSSARY

canals rivers that have been made by people

communist someone who believes everything (work, land, money) should be shared out equally between everyone

coniferous forest trees that keep their leaves all year

desert a hot dry place with little water where hardly anything can grow

erupt when a volcano throws out ash and lava (melted rock from under the earth's surface)

exports things that are sold to other countries

goods things people make

government people who run the country

nuclear power energy that can be used to make electricity

plain a large flat area of land

pollution dirt in the air, water or on land

public transport buses, taxis or trains that can be used by anyone who can pay the fare

revolution when the people in a country get rid of the rulers

tourist someone who visits a place on holiday

volcano a mountain that sometimes throws out ash and melted rock

INDEX

animals 9
arts 29

borders and coastlines 4

communist government 5, 18, 28

families 12–13, 16–17
farming 7, 14–15, 16
festivals 28, 29
flag 5
food and drink 13, 17, 19, 20–1

goods made in Russia 22–3

history 5
holidays and time off 27

industry 11, 22, 23

languages 30

money 30
Moscow 4, 11, 12–13, 24, 25, 29, 30

mountains and volcanoes 6

plants 9
pollution 11, 23
population 30
public transport 24, 25

railways 24, 25
religions 28, 30
rivers and lakes 7
roads 24

shopping 18–19
Siberia 7, 25
sports 26
St Petersburg 10, 24, 30
steppes 7, 9

tourism 4, 10, 19
towns and cities 10–11, 25, 30

tundra and taiga 9

weather 8